THE UNUSUAL JOURNEY OF A NATIONAL SERVICE MAN

By Philip Annetts

The Unusual Journey of a National Service Man
Edition 1

Copyright 2019 Philip Annetts

Green Salmon Publishing

All rights reserved.

No part of this book may be reproduced in any form without the prior permission in writing of the author, except for brief quotations used for promotion or in reviews.

CONTENTS

	Page No.
Reporting For Duty	1
I'm In the Army	7
Off to War!	11
Korea	17
Tokyo	21
Back to the War	27
Fighting for our Lives	31
Time to Regroup	33
Leaving Korea	39
Going Home	43
Reunions	47
The Epilogue	57

FOREWORD

This is a true account of a teenage boy, who had completed an apprenticeship in the plumbing and heating trade between 1945 and 1950, and knew that for the next 18 months of his life he must do his National Service for King and Country. As the story unfolds you will find that this soldier had a few more experiences than that of many National Service Personnel.

REPORTING FOR DUTY

Joining the army didn't ring any alarm bells for me. My friends had done, or were doing their National Service or like myself awaiting further orders. Conscription was 18 months, with a possibility of serving in Germany, Hong Kong, Malaya or somewhere in the UK, such as Catterick, Blandford Forum or Salisbury Plain. One of my mates had just completed his national service at Southern Command as a dispatch rider, his posting just 2 miles from his own front door step, at Wilton.

I was 18 years old in late 1949 when I passed the medical and I had just completed a 5 year apprenticeship as a plumber and heating engineer. I lived at home with my mother, step dad and two sisters in a small council house in Laverstock, a small village on the outskirts of Salisbury Wiltshire. I had recently met a girl, Sylvia and had been dating her for a few months. The winter came and went.

So on 9th March 1950 I received my orders, which were to report to Bulford Camp, about 10 miles from my home. I caught the local bus out to Bulford and on the bus was a chap from Basingstoke named Jack Heward. He was a tall guy with very distinct red hair. He had come by train to Salisbury. I didn't know we were going to the same place until we walked through the gates and up to the guard room to report in. We were told to go to a certain block and await further orders. We chatted with the other chaps as they came in throughout the morning, until there were about 20 of us in the block. As time went by about 20 others went into the block opposite. At Mid-day we were marched down to the dining hall for our first army meal.

I'm the 2nd on the left

After lunch it all started, documentation, kit issue, bedding etc. We all seemed to be running around like headless chickens having all this kit dumped onto us then, back to the barrack room. Little did I know that our platoon sergeant had overheard me say to Jack that I had done a summer camp with our local army cadet force, so I was told to take the bed next to the door as I was to become the section leader. It didn't mean much, only to help the slower lads with the laying out of their kit for inspections and making sure the place was always clean and tidy. Everything was proceeding well, marching, rifle drills, obstacle courses and target shooting. I didn't find the training hard, it disciplined the group and I felt pretty good, a lot fitter than before.

Here I am marching around the square at the barracks

It was quite easy for me to get up when reveille sounded as I was an early riser anyway. Rivalry between our two blocks was highly competitive in all aspects of our ten weeks training and with hindsight I believe we came out more proud of ourselves. Our instructors were either very pleased with the group 50/05 or just glad to get rid of us. (50/05 meant we were the fifth intake into the army in 1950). We were being trained by the Hampshire Regiment and were coming to the end of our ten week training, when we were all told to take our jackets to the tailors and have the Hampshire flashes put on them. We had been told that the regiment was being awarded the Freedom of the City of Portsmouth and our two squads were to make up the numbers as they were under strength.

We were transported down to Portsmouth in 3 ton trucks and slept under canvas the night prior to the parade, not the best conditions to look your best next day. However, the parade went very well. We marched through Pompey to the Guildhall where the dignitaries did their thing with drawn out speeches. Then with bayonets fixed we marched off towards Southsea, where we disbanded and came back to Bulford.

A Platoon photo - Here's me with Jack directly behind.

During my first week's training I had asked if I could go for a trade's test, seeing that I had just completed 5 years' apprenticeship in the plumbing and heating trade. If it worked out I could probably get a transfer to the Royal Engineers. Jack had also applied as he had an apprenticeship in the carpentry trade. So we came to the completion of our ten weeks training and had a grand Passing out Parade in Salisbury and then went on a few days leave.

On returning to Bulford, I expected us all to be going our separate ways to army units far and wide, but no, much to our surprise they all went off to Roman Way Camp in Colchester to join the Gloucester Regiment. Meanwhile Jack and I continued an advanced training course, doing very similar tests we had done previously. Plus every other day we seemed to be doing headquarters guard duty. When I asked how long before the tests, I was told anything up to 3 months.

After being told this I thought, "Damn this for a game of soldiers. I think I'll ask if I can join the rest of the gang." I told Jack of my intentions and he said. "If you're going, I'm coming with you". We went to the Adjutants Officer and asked permission to join the rest. Not bad I thought, only fifteen months to do, not too far to travel on leave and with that we were told to get our gear, given our train passes and off we went. Goodbye Bulford, hello Colchester.

I'M IN THE ARMY

On arriving at camp, when asked, we said we were interested in the regimental Signals and we were both lucky, so apart from a few parade ground bashes, we went back to the classroom learning all procedures relating to back-pack wireless sets and larger ones in vehicles. I settled down nicely to this way of life, and it seemed that weekend leave was going to work out very well, as it looked like I could expect leave about every three weeks. However, out of the blue orders came for 1 company and a few Signals, myself included, and we were bundled into trucks and off we went to Milden Hall, Suffolk. We were sent to the airfield where we had to guard the perimeter as there were rumours that the IRA were attempting to damage the Super Fortress aircraft stationed there over the weekend. Anyway, nothing happened so back to camp on Monday. That was goodbye to my weekend leave, back to the classroom again so I thought.

But no, Smithfield Marketers decided to go on strike so they called upon the army to take over. Jack and I were in the squad of men who were ordered to go, so off we went to London. Jack was quite happy about this as his relations lived nearby. We arrived of all places at the Tower of London and were shown to our sleeping quarters 'The Stables', where we had to make our own paillasses filled with straw to sleep on. It was fun and hilarious with all the banter going on. Off to Smithfield's Market at first light. Some lads went straight to the docks unloading frozen sheep carcases and bringing them back to be weighed by a few more lads, including myself. Then others took them to the butcher's shops around the city in 3 ton trucks. After this, we all went back to the Tower for a meal and clean up, then up to the Elephant and Castle in the evenings for a nice beer. Jack managed to contact his cousins and we met up with them at their local pub. This went on for a few days until the strike ended, and we returned to Colchester just in time for our weekend leave. The weekend leave seemed to fly by so quickly, seeing my girlfriend, parents and my future in-laws, and a visit to the cinema on the Saturday evening. Before I knew it, it was time to get the 6.15pm train, with never enough time to say all you wanted to say.

I thought that things had settled down calmly again, and time was going by quickly. I was very contented the ways things were shaping out. However, on arriving back from weekend leave the camp was in uproar. Squads of men were putting beds into empty barrack blocks, stores were issuing blankets etc., and of course, the camp was rife with rumours. It soon became clear that the reservists were being called up to bring the battalion up to full strength, but for what?

Within a few days we were all assembled in the gymnasium where Colonel Carne gave us the news that we were off to the Korean War. We were part of the 29th Independent Brigade, which included the Royal Ulster Rifles and the Northumberland Fusiliers, but first we were going off to Norfolk for extensive training. ***This wasn't supposed to happen!*** I had settled down to a nice routine, comfortable billets, and easy classroom tests plus a few square bashes a week and a good roster for weekend leave. Well that knocked that on the head!

We were now at a tented area at South Bodney near Thetford Norfolk and then it started; route marches with full kit, plus all weapons, mock battles, rifle ranges and much more. The weather was very warm during the day making the marches very exhausting; at night it was getting chilly. We were now into autumn, washing and shaving with cold water, it wasn't very pleasant. We eventually went back to Colchester and were given seven days leave. Returning back to camp I assumed that being National Service I would probably go to another regiment in another brigade, but the CO got all National Service personnel back in the Gym to say that our National Service was extended from 18 months to 2 years and that all men would be going with the battalion. **Well that was a bolt out of the blue.**

This was not what I was expecting. I felt rather demoralised. How was I going to tell the family at home? What a shock! I thought that as the battalion were off to Korea, that we would be a bag of misfits, left behind and scattered far and wide. Well now we knew so we just had to get on with it. I was told that a few of us were staying behind as a rear-guard party to clear up any outstanding jobs. So off went the battalion leaving this skeleton crew behind. In a few days we were sent home for 7 days embarkation leave, and nearing the end of the leave a message came to take a further 7 days and report back on the 3rd November. A very nice surprise, but eventually I had to go back which was a terrible wrench, not knowing when I would see my girlfriend and family again. So I took a train back to Colchester late evening only to find we were off to Southampton at first light.

OFF TO WAR!

Waiting for us, tied to the dock, was HMT Charlton Star, the smallest of the troop carriers. We set sail on the day before firework night, little knowing what fireworks lay ahead and that some of us would never see the shores of England again. I was surprised to hear Jack say "I don't think I'll be home again". We all gave him a good rollicking for being so morbid and nothing more was said on the subject.

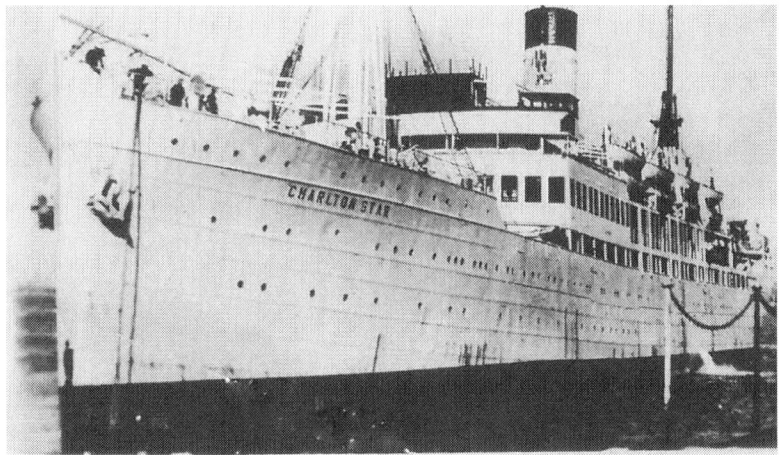

The Charlton Star which took us to Singapore from Southampton docks.

So our long journey began. The Bay of Biscay was a nightmare. The troughs in the sea were so deep that the propeller was often out of the water sending terrific vibrations throughout the ship. It calmed down while travelling down the Atlantic Ocean and we entered the Mediterranean Sea. Unfortunately, we had someone taken ill so we lay off of Gibraltar and a tender came out and took him off.

The Med was like a millpond, and the physical training instructors kept us on our toes - exercises, team obstacle races with scrambling nets laid out on the decks which we had to crawl under, followed by climbing ropes to ring a bell. There was also a small pool on deck, which had a rope secured under the water. We had to jump in the pool, go under the rope, then scramble up more ropes to get out. It kept you fit, and no one was excused from the fitness classes.

Arriving at Port Said in Egypt, we anchored for the first time while we took on drinking water. Lots of little boats swarmed around the ship, some had carpets for sale and others had fruit. It was good fun bartering. I bought a pineapple and shared it around. Up anchor and we were off through the Suez Canal and across the Red Sea to Ceylon, now known as Sri Lanka. At Colombo we went ashore for the first time, very warm but it was good to stand on terra firma again. We had just a few hours break, before we were back on board, and sailing to our next stop, Singapore.

At Singapore we said goodbye to a group of our shipmates who were joining the Devonshire Regiment in Malaya, much ribbing going on about it being a home posting compared to where we were going, and off they went. Shortly after they had left dockside there were more orders given for some other men to disembark, including myself, so we gathered our kit and proceeded ashore.

We formed up on the dockside and were told to remove our boots and put on our PT shoes. Soon after, we were marched off to another quay, where we saw this gigantic P&O liner The

Chusan. She was on her maiden voyage to Hong Kong and we were told to go aboard, up the gangway to be greeted by stewards who showed us to our cabins. It was luxury the likes of which I, and I'm sure the others had never experienced before. As we pulled away from the harbour, there were banners waving, bands playing, fireworks and miles of bunting.

Down below we had two men per cabin. Jack and I shared a cabin. We had orange juice brought to us in the mornings before going to our own area for meals. We were restricted as to where we could go on board and on what deck, but it was still luxury. No Physical Training Instructors (PTIs) in sight. This lasted I'm sure for three days, until we arrived at Hong Kong. What a fan fare of horns blowing, bunting and crowds in their thousands who had come to see the largest ship ever to dock in Hong Kong. During the day we disembarked and were taken across the water to Kowloon. This was mainland China, as Hong Kong is an island. At the time Hong Kong and the New Territories were under UK rule. Well what can I say, these last few days had been absolute luxury, but I soon came back to

reality when I saw a couple of 3 ton trucks waiting. About 20 of us were taken into the new territories, approximately 30 miles, where we came to the headquarters of the Wiltshire Regiment.

They had a small tented area ready for us, not quite the comfort we had got used to in the last 3 days, but that' life. However, we were told this was for one night only, as the next morning we would be off again.

Luckily for us it remained quite dry. So after breakfast we got back on the trucks and made our way back to Kowloon and boarded a light aircraft carrier The Unicorn, which was a floating workshop for the far eastern fleet carrying spare parts to and fro, where we had to share quarters with the crew. It was very cramped, but we tried to keep out of their way. We set sail midday, had a meal, then a new experience. We had to go and get a hammock each and were shown how to hang them over the mess decks. I found the hammock surprisingly comfortable, but things got pretty hairy as we made our way through the Straits of Formosa (now Taiwan). We ran into a typhoon, and being a small carrier we were tossed about like a cork. The mess decks were running in water, the aircraft in the holds were damaged and to add to the confusion, emergency crews were at work, something to do with a buckled bow plate. The rough seas continued for several days and stayed with us until we reached Sasebo in Southern Japan. *What was going on??* I thought we were going to Korea to join our regiment The Glosters, but it seems someone had other ideas. Anyway we were glad to get off that floating tin can.

Now we got on a train which took us across country to the coastal town of Kure (now known as Kobe). Kobe had been a submarine base during WW2. From here we were bussed out to a small village called Hiro, where we were billeted in an old Japanese army camp. This was made up of a few sturdy huts which made good sleeping quarters for us and a mess room with long benches where we had our meals. The place had been virtually unused since the end of WW2. We had been there only about 48 hours when we were told we were going on a long trek up into the mountains.

We eventually got to a small encampment and told we were to help set up a battle school, an extensive training area for reinforcements that would be ready then to join the 29th Brigade in Korea. Work was going on – making obstacle courses, rifle ranges, wireless training, points etc. Some of us could find ourselves lucky and be on the permanent staff. Sounded great, but it wasn't to be. Within days the gang I'd been with since leaving Southampton were called back to Hiro only to be told we were flying out to Korea the next day. I thought to myself it was about time we caught up with our mates in the Signal Platoon, shouldn't be long now.

KOREA

So up we went to the airstrip next morning where we boarded an Australian Dakota. On taxiing for take-off someone said, "Where's the door?" A crewman said "There ain't no door mate. You'll find out why later on". There was no door just the space where one should have been. As we approached our landing strip he said the plane would almost stop, but just enough for us to jump out (reason for no door). This we did, picked up our kit and ran to cover and watched from a long trench along the airstrip, as the aircraft took straight off. We were told later that often the guerrillas in the hills had been mortaring the airstrip and that's why everything was kept moving.

Well, 7 weeks from leaving Southampton, we were here at last and what a place – snow, Siberian winds, heaps of rubble everywhere and aircraft with broken wings or upside down. What a mess. What really caught my eye were the streams of refugees heading south in a continuous line. It seemed like mile after mile, as far as the eye could see.

It wasn't long before some trucks came and off we went. After a short drive we came to an open area where we were told to form up into three ranks and an officer from the Royal Ulster Rifles explained that due to a great loss of men in the Happy Valley battle, we were joining their battalion on secondment – in other words, until their reinforcements arrived and we would re-join the Glosters. With that a sergeant came along splitting the ranks into groups and as he came to our rank, Jack and I were standing side by side and he cut us off right between us. Thus I went to Charlie Company and Jack went to Able Company. With just a quick "See you later", we were off and that was the last I saw of him.

Our group went by truck over to Charlie Company, where we were put into platoons. No wireless set now, just a rifle and bayonet. We were in reserve where the battalion were having a much earned rest after the recent battle. Our job was to guard a bridge which refugees, who I had seen earlier, were coming over. Guerrillas were getting through with these poor people; even women with babies on their backs were carrying grenades under their babies, or in their clothing. Therefore, each person was searched for hidden arms and grenades. This went on all day, searching and searching, but as night fell the bridge closed until the next morning leaving the refugees on the far side. One night noises were heard on the bridge and it turned out to be a young tot. Next morning some of the refugees were found frozen to death. Maybe the tot's mother was among the dead, as no one came to claim him. He was handed over to be taken to a child refuge somewhere south.

Patrols up to the bridge and guard duties were dark, freezing cold and tense. The sound of the ice cracking on the river set my nerves on edge, until I realised what it was - never knowing whether there was someone there.

One night on guard duties, I was aware that snow and ice had formed in my right boot and my trousers were stuck to my leg. My foot felt numb and stamping my foot didn't make any feeling come back. Back at our platoon area our sergeant helped take my boot off and the pain was excruciating as the pressure of my boot was released. Frostbite had got me in my right foot and up to my calf. I was taken back to one of the MASH hospitals, where they confirmed the situation. From there I was taken to Kimpo airfield, where I was put on a stretcher and taken aboard an American Constellation aircraft. I was strapped into a frame and flown back to Japan.

Well into the flight I could see it was getting darker outside, so looking out I saw a film of oil appear across the window. There were a few others who had noticed it too, when the pilot came over the intercom to say that one engine had to be shut down. Shortly after this we landed and when leaving the plane, I could see the whole side of the fuselage was dripping in oil and the smell was terrible. Had it caught fire, I think that would have been our lot.

TOKYO

I finished up in the annexe of the Tokyo General Hospital, and as I was wheeled into the ward, all I could see were two rows of beds with arched domes on them. Then from behind these domes, arms went up and some said 'Hi Buddy'. It was only after I had a similar dome placed over my legs to keep the bedding off of them that I could see we were all in the same boat.

Tokyo General Hospital

They were all Americans in the ward. The guy on my left had to lay face down as he had lost his left buttock through being hit with a cannon shell while diving for cover. He would scream in agony every time they removed all the gauze from his wound and applied fresh dressings. On the other side was a lad that had shot himself through the left leg whilst cleaning his officer's revolver. Most of the others were recovering from shrapnel wounds. I know now why they called the trains carrying the wounded 'Blood Wagons'.

I had very little in the way of toiletries and so the American patients had a whip round, they sent a nurse over with some dollars that they had collected, which I was very grateful for. With the money I got one of the orderlies to go to the 'PX' for razor blades etc. 'PX' or Postal Exchanges was similar to our NAAFI.

There was another Englishman in the next ward, Wilfred from the Middlesex Regiment. He had gone back behind the front line to the rear echelon to collect the mail. He had stopped on his way and lit a fire for a brew, which happened to be right over a live grenade, and he had shrapnel in his legs. With him was a Frenchman named Paul, another frost bite victim. He had lost his fingers from both hands leaving just his thumbs with two stumps. Wilf and Paul came in and sat around my bed most days. I think they came just to look out of the window, for in the distance you could see Mt Fujian. We had a pilot in our ward who had been shot down, but luckily rescued. Unfortunately, a cannon shell had taken half his right leg off above the knee. The poor bloke kept asking for a mirror so he could see the damage, but no one was allowed to give him one. He was shortly going to have his leg amputated.

But the most pitiful of all was this lad about my age. He had been shot in the head and it had taken both his eyes clean out. I still see him there screaming 'I can't see. What's happened to me, somebody tell me'. He was about to be flown back to the States. It was then for the first time in my National Service, I felt completely alone, totally dependent on others, and in a foreign land, in an American/Japanese hospital, unable to walk and a foot and leg as black as a burnt newspaper.

A doctor saw me and told me I would be started on a series of injections at intervals of two hours. I had this oil based penicillin injected first into my buttocks, then my upper leg, then my arms and each time leaving large bumps as it was slow to disperse. I did have a few hours respite between midnight and six in the morning. This went on for a few days. Then one morning two doctors came to my bed and one stuck a needle in my calf, but there was no response. I knew they were concerned about gangrene being present. After a further 36 hours they came back, and again in went the needle. This time my God did I jump, which made me use a few choice words. This came as a great relief to them and myself, as one of the orderlies said if gangrene had set in, amputation was the likelihood.

The British Ambassador came to see me and gave me a 10 dollar bill, so I was able to get some toiletries sent up from the PX. One afternoon we were told to sit up in our beds and along came some brass hats with a junior officer carrying a tray with Purple Heart medals. This is a medal Americans get if wounded in action. When they got to me they were just about to pin a

Purple Heart to my pyjama jacket, when someone said, "He's from England, UK, not New England", so they quickly by-passed me and went on their way.

One afternoon the walking casualties and I were put into wheelchairs, taken down to the ambulances and taken to the Tokyo Opera House. We were given pride of place in the circle, with cameras flashing in their hundreds. Movie cameras going to and fro. Then we sat through the opera "The Mikado", that went on for what seemed like hours. During the interval the Geisha girls came off stage and stood in front of our seats and handed each of us a large bouquet of flowers. On arriving back at the hospital I gave my flowers to one of the nurses, but kept the ribbon that was around them to send home.

After a few more days I was told I was moving to Kure, to the Australian Hospital. So I got issued with a brand new American uniform, and with a crutch to help me along, a small kit bag with my personal kit in and a further bag with medical notes and medicines, I was taken to the station and put on a train to Kure. This again was a new experience. I had never been on a foreign train on my own. I remember passing though the old capital Kyoto. Kure was the next main station and on arriving I was picked up by ambulance and taken to the Australian run hospital. The first person I saw was the Regimental Sergeant Major. "What the hell are you doing in that uniform", he bellowed. "Get it off", so I was taken to the stores, where I was issued with all new kit. My recovery had been very successful, but some physio was still needed. "No need to stay in hospital" they said. "We're sending you to a convalescent camp on the Island of Mia-jima, just off the mainland."

So on the ferry I went. I didn't know quite what to expect but was pleasantly surprised to see this camp amongst the trees. It was so peaceful with its tranquil atmosphere.

Mia-jima harbour 1951

Apparently Mia-jima is where in WW2 the Kamikaze pilots spent their last few days before taking off on a one way ticket.Physio was reduced as I could now exercise quite freely myself, sitting around relaxing, sipping juices and a few beers. I got one week of this. The island had a good shopping area, and there were also temples everywhere to explore.

Like all things, my week in Mia-jima came to an end, so I went back to Kure and then onto Hiro, the Japanese camp I had left earlier. I was told I would be going back to Korea the next day so I got busy writing my last letters home, telling them what was happening. At this time my mind was working overtime. Questions kept popping up in my head. Have all my mates returned to the Gloster Battalion as we were only on secondment? The Rifles reinforcements must have arrived by now!! Had they forgotten me? After 10 weeks of hospitalisation and recuperation I boarded the train at Kobe and made my way down to Sasebo, and found the boat that was taking returning soldiers back to Korea, mostly Americans.

BACK TO THE WAR

It was an old banana boat with just slats to rest on. However, we eventually arrived at Pusan, where I found our Military Police and got instructions to catch a train to Tague. What a journey. We were often pulled into sidings to let ambulance trains through, known as blood wagons, but after a day and a half we did eventually get to Tague. I spent a few hours in the waiting area before a truck arrived and took me back to HQ of the Rifles at Yondongpo a suburb of Seoul.

I got back to Charlie Company to find my old mates still there. I was then told we were now being transferred permanently to the Rifles and would spend the rest of our time with them. So a lot of questions were answered straight away. Now the month of March, the weather was quite nice - not the minus 30 degrees that it had been when I had left in January, which the lads here had gone through.

Then came the bad news, Ray one of our original Bulford gang came across and told me that Jack had been killed a few weeks earlier. A mortar bomb exploded right by the side of him, killing him straight away and some others were injured. My thoughts flashed back to the day we left Southampton when Jack said he wouldn't be back….

Things were on the move and we were to advance to a large range of hills across the valley. Our company was ordered to push forward onto a mountain range. The going was tough with a heavy wooded and rocky climb and we had to halt that night on a shoulder below the peak. No one slept that night, 100% stand to and at first light we moved onto the far side overlooking the Imjin River. The enemy had moved back across the river and into the hills beyond, so we dug in and made ourselves as comfortable as was possible. I must say at this time I received all my back mail as previous to this being on the move on my own, it was always a catch up situation.

Back to reality, the weather now was beautiful - lovely warm days and we were patrolling down to the river. We had a lovely view from our hill top position and many senior officers came to our O.P. with binoculars searching the hills on the north bank for any movement. Being in the front line, i.e. no one between you and the enemy, can be very daunting, even when it seems not a lot is going on. Somewhere on both sides there was patrolling - sections of men out in no-man's land trying to glean information as to how strong the opposition were in any part of the line and always hoping to take prisoners.

It was now early April and we'd been here for a while when we had orders to cross the river and occupy a hill known as 194. I, with everyone else, carried plenty of ammunition, Bren gun magazines and grenades. As it turned out the enemy had moved back further so everything went OK. Once there we quickly dug in and wired for defence. We were quiet here but the Yanks to the east were having a rough time. We stayed here for about 5 days; very tense knowing you had the river between you and safer ground on the other side. The enemy were not very happy with us being on their side of the river and at night sent patrols to sniff around to see what we were all about. Every night the enemy would probe one part of our defence or another just trying to find out what we were doing there. On one occasion they got into a section, but were soon dealt with leaving several dead bodies, but taking their wounded away with them, as trails of blood could be seen forward of our position, Then we were relieved by a Belgian Battalion with whom we left loads of spare ammo which they were most pleased to accept and we went into Brigade reserve getting a well-earned rest and clean up, or so we thought.

FIGHTING FOR OUR LIVES

After two days rumours started that the enemy were trying to find ways of crossing the river, but had been repulsed, but on the night of 22nd April all hell was let loose. The enemy attacked in force right along the front. We moved forward to the hills overlooking the valley. We had no idea what was going on in other parts of the brigade. Things were really hotting up and our company moved onto a ridge to stop the enemy slipping around behind us. If anything moved it was fired upon in order to keep their heads down. This we did until the morning of the 25th when we were told we were withdrawing, we were late leaving our position, and our defensive fire caused casualties with no way of getting them out. An officer and medic gallantly stayed behind to wait for an ambulance but the ambulance was knocked out on the way up and never reached them.

We were late leaving our hill position and moved down onto the valley floor and started our way down route 11. *Big mistake!* The Chinese were already in the valley so it was every man for himself, diving into ditches, firing back and running to get behind little nulls in the ground. We were fighting for our lives! After what seemed like hours I got to a decent bit of cover where our Platoon Sergeant said "get rid of your small pack, just keep your rifle, ammunition, bandoliers and water bottle." The ditch was filled with small packs with everyone's private belongings in them, including my letters I'd received from my girlfriend and family back home. We began to bunch up as others were coming through, so I took off with 4 other chaps around the side of a small hill and dived into the first gulley.

I then said "Let's make our way up the gulley and go south just under the skyline". Those hills were very steep and high. On climbing the gulley I got to where it started to level out then suddenly to my horror I saw a machine gun pointing right down on us. I raised my rifle above my head and let them know we were there, when up from behind the machine gun, a black American beckoned us to come forward. When we got to him he said, "We've been waiting for you guys all day and we're just pulling out". Much to our surprise a medic who was with us said he felt he must go back as there were so many wounded needing help. We watched him walk back down the gully and out of sight.

We hurried on South and we managed to get a lift on a centurion tank for a short while, then a long march until we reached a holding position where we were told to dig in with what tools we could find and we got some food for the first time that day. Just before midnight we left our holding position and marched a further seven miles, where transport arrived and took us south through the night back to the old Japanese depot where we had been before moving up to the Imjin river. I managed to get some breakfast, then I must have fallen asleep for hours. We had survived the day!

TIME TO REGROUP

Days afterwards, we learnt what a hell of a battle we had been in and how lucky I was to have fought in it and survived. At the time I got to write home to my girlfriend and family to let them know I was OK. The newspapers back home must have been packed with stories. I found out later that my girlfriend's workmates would not let her see the newspapers until they had read the casualty list. On 29th April, *my girlfriend's birthday*, we moved back onto the line in a reserve position, best we'd ever had with a football pitch, green lawns and orchards in blossom, but within 48 hours we went in to relieve the Fusiliers on the Han River bank – a lot of digging and wiring, I recall.

At this point, I moved to Company HQ signal section which meant when on patrol, I carried a 31 radio set on my back or 62 set mounted in the company jeep or carrier.

Once again we started patrolling well in front of our defensive line and found no resistance. In fact the enemy had moved back across the Imjin river and within a few weeks we were back overlooking the river in what had been the Glosters' position. The Glosters were almost wiped out during the battle. We had the thankless task of removing dead bodies from the trenches where some had been partly covered; others were just pieces laying around. These were reburied and the war graves commission notified.

Once more life settled down to patrolling down to the river. Summer was really hot and mostly uneventful on our part of the front line. I spent my spare time writing letters to my girlfriend, mother and grandmother. I was lucky in the fact that my girlfriend wrote regularly to me. We had a couple of lads with us where their mail became less frequent and then the dreaded 'Dear John' letters came. They were absolutely gutted and took some time to get over it, drowning their sorrows in beer. Being thousands of miles from home, they could do nothing about it. Poor devils.

It wasn't all doom and gloom, in some instances when we were static for a while, we'd have a bulldozer come up and scratch out a soccer field or small rifle range or running trails. Thereby inter-company teams could compete against each other or other parts of the brigade, such as Artillery or Engineers sides.

The reservists we had with us were great blokes; some had been in the European War and told us their stories. One, we called Dusty, got out of Dunkirk on a small boat, then onto North Africa fighting Rommel, and then onto Italy to fight in the battle for Monte Casino. Then with only a few months left of his army reserve time left to do, he was called up again for Korea. We became friends and a few years later he came to live in our village with his niece.

Then a few of us were told to get our kit together – we were off for 5 days rest and recuperation leave in Japan. We flew into Tokyo and had billets at the Ibishu Australian camp. Showers and new kit were supplied and then out to taste a few beers.

Looking in the shops was all new for me and I came across a place where if you bought something they would ship it home for you. I bought a Japanese tea set and had it sent to my girlfriend Sylvia. Sometime later Sylvia wrote to say it had arrived and we still have it today. Five days soon passed and back once more to the front line. Things started to get busy with patrols across the river, mostly carried on tanks, then on foot to the range hills further in. We were seldom challenged but the odd things told you they were watching our every move.

Being a wireless operator in the Infantry was very rewarding and gave me a lot of self-satisfaction. For instance, in some circumstances, tanks were used as our artillery. On one patrol an enemy look out bunker had been spotted on the opposite hill, so after giving the co-ordinates to the tanks, our platoon officer asked for one round open fire. Watching for impact he said to tell them to raise 300 and the result was the shells crashed into the timber made bunker, leaving a distinctive V in the ridge line of the hill.

On another occasion the company went onto the next range of hills. Where upon the major said, 'Come with me', and leaving the rest of the company in position we stepped out, just the two of us and proceeded to walk up the hill until it started to level out. At which point he got out his binoculars and had a good look around. While we were doing this shells were whistling just over our heads and crashing into the valley just ahead. He said, 'Are they going out or coming in', and I told him they were ours. 'OK, let's go back, that's far enough' he said, so we turned and re-joined our company about a quarter of a mile back and continued our company patrol. No casualties and a very relieved wireless operator.

Patrolling was very hard on the nerves at the best of times, but radio operators had the additional noise of the static rush through the earphone and at night or during tense situations you thought you could be heard 100 yards away. Out in no-man's land, during standing patrols, it was always tense. There were other times when you were on the other end, at Company HQ, listening to patrols where you had probably been the day before.

We lived on the hills at night, protected by trenches and barbed wire. The barbed wire had tin cans containing stones attached to it, to act as a warning system. A very good alarm of course unless some animal decided to be nosey. We made canvas shelters just behind the trenches to sleep in, with normal guard duties each night. We lived on American 'C' rations when on the move, otherwise, 15cwt trucks brought fresh meals up to us or as near as they could get. Then it was man-handled up the rest of the way. There was always something to do, like lugging wireless batteries up to the position, making the trenches just that bit deeper and killing the odd rat crawling about the trenches.

Summer was coming to an end and someone decided our line would move to the range of hills we had been patrolling across the Imjin. This went fairly smoothly, until we started patrols forward again, and then things really got nasty on one hill in particular. We were mortared all day long on our observation hill called 'How'. One bomb landed on the side of my trench and shrapnel ripped the compete stock off my rifle, and my radio slid back on top of myself and our patrol officer, lucky us. The enemy mortar crew were so well hidden, but were so close that you could hear the officer give the command to fire. Patrols were going to the hill every day and just 2 days after our close shave a mortar dropped into the trench and killed 2 of our company. All along the line it was getting nasty, but while this was going on rumours started that we were going to be relieved by the Royal Norfolk Regiment. However, before this could happen we were told we were going to advance and take the next range of hills in what would be known as Operation Commando. We had the task of taking the left flank of hills and to dig in forming a new front line. Everything went well and after a few days a battalion of French Canadians came up to get familiar with the area and took over. So at last light we could pull back behind the line, but on standby should there be any trouble. All went well and the Royal Norfolks came to our area and we handed over our equipment and we went back across the Imjim River for the last time, and travelled down to Pusan. This took us a couple days.

LEAVING KOREA

Our advance party had erected a tented area for each company on the side of the hill overlooking the sea. Unfortunately that night we had a hurricane with torrential rain which flattened our Bivouacs and soaked all our kit and equipment. We all looked like drowned rats in the morning.

After the hurricane.

However, we managed to get dried out during the next 3 days and on 23rd October 1951 we went down to the docks and boarded the HMT Empire Halladale and disembarked at Hong Kong on the 27th October 1951.

On board the Empire Halladale.

As we pulled away I looked back with mixed feelings, glad to have got out alive and sad for my Bulford mates that weren't so lucky. Eleven months since leaving Hong Kong the first time, we were now back again at Kowloon.

We went by trucks into the New Territories about 30 miles to a village called Fanling where our company were accommodated in Nissen huts. During the Hurricane before we left Korea, the rain had got into our company files and therefore, many would have to be copied where possible, to bring the records back up to date. Seeing that I had been in Company HQ, I was asked if I would take on the job.

Fanling Company Office.

40

I accepted and moved into the Company Office, and had my own area where I could work undisturbed.

So it was just the occasional march round the Territories to keep fit, and at weekends I went with mates down to Kowloon or across to Hong Kong on the ferry to have a few beers. Life was great and Korea seemed a million miles away. Christmas came and went with great bottle parties leading up to the New Year. During the Christmas period I walked over to the Wiltshire Regiment and found my future brother in law Eric who had just arrived from the UK, telling me how it was at home. I now felt excited knowing I would be back there quite soon.

GOING HOME

Checking the office mail one morning, one contained all of 50/05 group names on with instructions to be ready to leave for Blighty at the weekend. I now knew it wouldn't be long before we would be heading home. When the news came the excitement grew. At last, I still couldn't believe it. Our Company Major took me to one side, shook my hand and said "Well done" and wished me good luck. Then I stood before the Adjutant who also wished me good luck; he had been our battalion wireless officer in Korea. So the weekend arrived and with a quick cheerio I left Fanling with what was left of our Bulford gang and went down to Kowloon where laying at anchor was the HMT Empire Orwell. This most beautiful ship (well she was to me) was going to take me home. We all went aboard and shortly after set sail for Singapore, where we picked up more men going home for demob. I did not recognize any of them that had out with us.

It was at this time I broke a tooth break and I was in agony having a sleepless, painful night. So next morning I reported sick; I'm fairly sure our ship's doctor had not carried out many extractions for he fussed about with a table full of tools before coming to a decision on what to use. To start with the injections were inserted with reluctance and after a while he took the plunge and yanked the tooth out. What a relief! I'm not sure who was more relieved, him or me, but all was well once more as we sailed for home.

As we approached the Suez Canal we were told to mount machine guns along port and starboard sides as the Egyptians were likely to throw grenades onto the decks. However, we passed through the canal with no incidents and did not stop at Port Said, but sailed on to Algiers where we took on supplies, especially water. We left Algiers, this being our last stop. The next few days seemed to drag, and then at last we were almost home. On coming into Southampton docks we were told to go to our lifeboat stations and to stay there until we had docked. This was because we were known as a light ship, which meant we were very low on water and supplies and if everyone had all gone dockside the ship would probably lean so far over that damage to the cranes and the ship was possible.

After being docked for about an hour we could at last go ashore if we had relations dockside. I could see my girlfriend together with my grandmother, uncle and friend, so I was very soon off the ship and into the arms of my girl and family. At long last I would hold her in my arms after fifteen months.

The morning orders of the day were posted up before we docked and much to my surprise I had to go to St Patricks Barracks in Ballymena in Northern Ireland to be demobbed, so I told my girl and family what had to happen before I would be home. I had thought I would go to Devizes in Wiltshire for that but no. So after an hour or so, I had to watch them leave the docks and head home having said cheerio and see you in a couple of days. I went back on board where I slept for one more night and caught a train next morning to Liverpool, then a ferry over to Belfast where we were trucked up to the barracks. The next morning I thought there would be kit checks and rail warrants handed out but no. The Adjutant said, "Seeing that you had 5 days leave in Japan, you'll have to do an extra 5 days here". I was gobsmacked; we just hung around doing nothing, but watched new recruits being put through the drills.

On the third day I went into the office (tongue in cheek) and said would it be possible to leave that night as I had one and a half days travelling to get home and to my surprise they said OK. So 8 of us caught the ferry back to Liverpool and from there I went to Birmingham, Bristol and then Devizes dropping off lads on the way down. At Devizes I was told to stop overnight and go home the next day. I didn't want to delay getting home so I managed to get a ride to the bus station that evening. I caught a bus home to Salisbury and just managed to get the last bus out to our village and there I was back home after what seemed a lifetime away.

My army life was not over and like all National servicemen there was a further 3 ½ years to do in the Territorial Army Reserves. After a few weeks I had orders to join "A" Company of the 4th Battalion of the Wiltshire Regiment which was situated in a drill hall in Salisbury. This is where drills were carried out and it also had a rifle range. Each year I had to do 2 weeks compulsory camp, mainly out on Salisbury Plain with the full battalion. In other words back in the army for a fortnight. I quickly came up through the ranks, so I signed on for a few more years gaining the rank of Sergeant. However, being married and having 2 children I felt I had enough of playing soldiers, so in 1958 I called it a day so my commitment to Queen and country was now at an end.

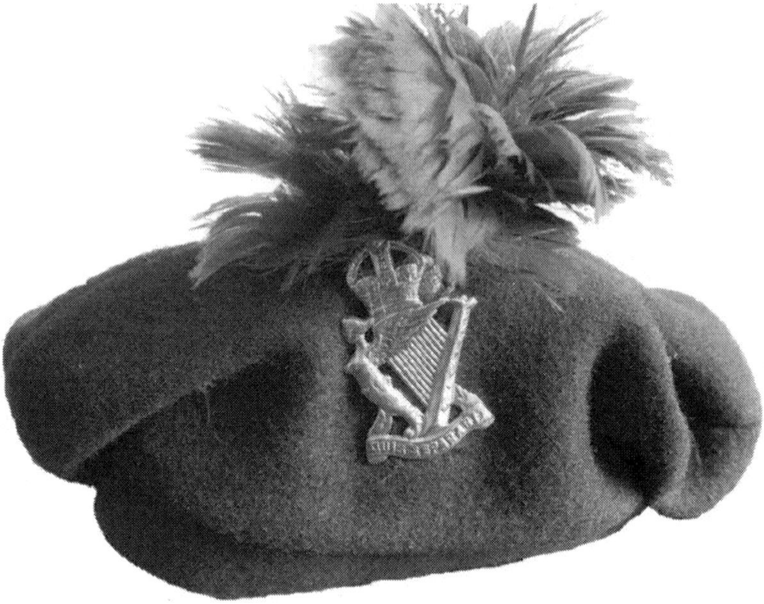

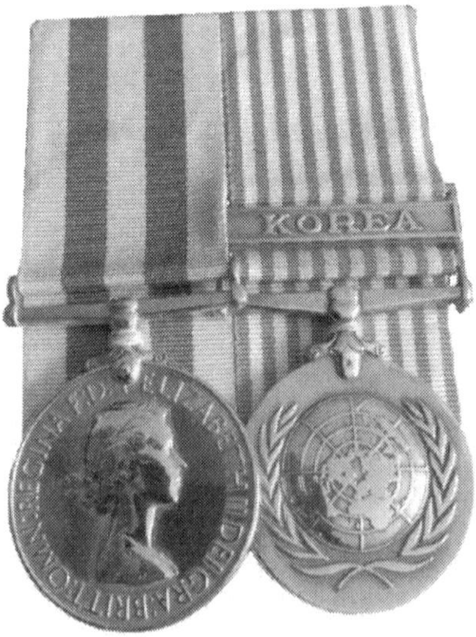
KOREA

REUNIONS

In recent years I have had the opportunity to visit South Korea twice.

The first was in 1983, it was the 30th anniversary of the end of the war. With an invitation from the Korean Veterans Association my wife and I along with 168 Veterans were flown by Korean airways to Seoul airport. We were transported in luxury coaches to the Walker Hill Hotel (named after General Walker, Commander UN Forces who was tragically killed in a motor accident on or near the spot where the hotel now stands).

We were taken around in coaches to visit many places where conflicts had taken place, with Parades at the Gloster Hill Memorial. Wherever we went we were applauded by the people who wanted to touch us and shake our hands – very heart warming.

We had a grand gala night the evening prior to departure where after a wonderful meal and entertainment each veteran was presented with the Ambassador for Peace medal and ribbon from the Korean Veterans Association.

One evening, we had a visit from Korean policeman asking for 'A' Company of the Glosters, as he had heard that some veterans were in town. Well Frank, one of our veterans, spoke up and the man introduced himself as a little orphaned boy who had been picked up and thrown on a soldier's back and became a chore boy for the Company until he was eventually dropped off at an orphanage run by nuns. Frank said "Are you

Kim?" to which he replied "Yes". Upon hearing this there were hugs, tears and kisses and when things cooled down he told us that from a chore boy in Frank's Company he became a high ranking policeman in Seoul.

That's me on the left and Frank on the right

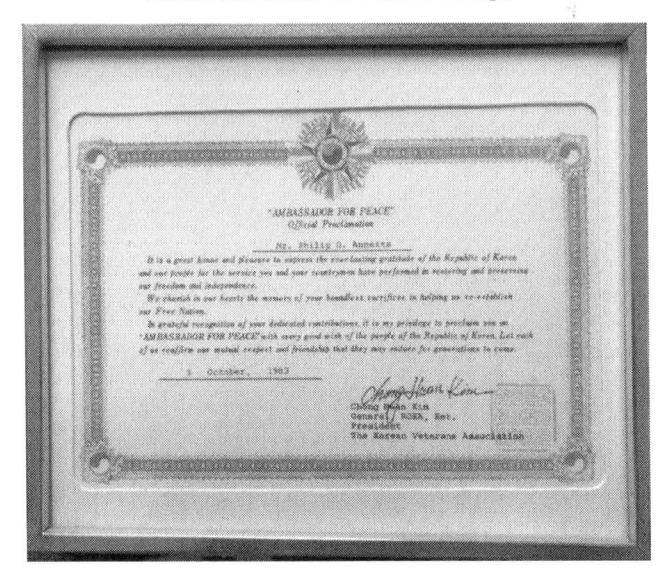

49

I visited Korea again in 2010 with my eldest son Stephen. My wife had just had a shoulder replacement operation, so could not travel, but insisted that I went. This time we stayed at the Lottie Hotel right in the centre of Seoul.

This year was the 60th anniversary of the outbreak of the Korean War. Our agenda every day was packed with places to visit, at every battlefield we had parades to mark this special occasion, dedicated to the countrymen who fought there. My most memorable day was when we caught the bullet train from Seoul to Pusan (now Busan) and went to the United Nations Cemetery where we held a Service of Remembrance for the 1000 British War dead. This took us an hour on the train, unlike the 2 days it took us by truck in 1951.

After the service we had time to wander. I found Jack's grave (right under the Union Jack) on which I placed two red roses, a very sad moment, but I was just pleased to see where he was laid to rest and say-

"Good bye old friend".

Jack's resting place

51

Two days before we were due to leave a volcano in Iceland erupted called Eyjafjallajökull and had spread dust into the atmosphere, thereby stopping aircraft from flying into England for six days. The hotel was fully booked, with new guests arriving on the day we should be leaving. The problem was solved by taking us across to Incheon to a brand new hotel right on the coast. We were well looked after and our hosts had planned excursions for us every day. Coastal Areas, Military Museums, even the big fish markets, plus we had plenty of free time to walk in their wonderful parks or swim in the pools. Each day we were in contact with home by email getting all the information. My daughter and son-in-law were stranded in Miami, for the same reason, so we had a three-way transmission going on.

One day we were asked to be at the hotel for dinner at six o clock and when we were all seated who should come in but the former Prime Minister, John Major. He was on a business tour of the Far East and on hearing we were in town, insisted on meeting us. He thanked us for our service during the war and after a short speech came round and shook us all by the hand, stopping to speak to most of us before leaving to catch a plane to Hong Kong.

After a few days the skies were clear again and so we said farewell to our wonderful South Korean Hosts and flew home to our loved ones.

> **Thank You**
> United Kingdom
>
> 60
>
> 60 YEARS OF COMMITMENT
> 60 YEARS OF FRIENDSHIP
>
> THE YEAR 2010 MARKS THE 60TH ANNIVERSARY OF THE OUTBREAK OF THE KOREAN WAR. THE PEACE, PROSPERITY AND LIBERTIES THAT WE CHERISH TODAY ARE BUILT ON YOUR SELFLESS SACRIFICES AND CONTRIBUTIONS. KOREA IS FOREVER INDEBTED AND WE WILL CONTINUE TO BUILD THE TRUST AND FRIENDSHIP BETWEEN OUR NATIONS.
>
> REPUBLIC OF KOREA

So here we are at the end of a story of a country boy who did service for his country come what may and came through with his head held high. Summing up my time in the army, it was 2 years where from day one you knew you were on your own – amongst other lads, yes, but we were all in the same boat as it were, so looking after number one was essential. The time spent in England with the Hampshire and the Gloucestershire Regiment's were with lads that were 99% from the Southern

Counties, like me. The shock came when I joined the Royal Ulster Rifles, for a start they were Light Infantry with a pace of 140 instead of the 120 pace of the heavy infantry I was used to. Accents were also a problem at the start, what with North and South Irish brogues together with North Country lads, but eventually got used to that. So from a peace time situation to a war zone fighting for my life it was horrendous and will live with me forever. I made many friends during my army career; unfortunately my best friend Jack was killed in action. Had he survived I'm sure we would have been friends for life, but it was not to be and that is why I believe that fate had been a big part in my life. Things happen for a reason, I'm sure of that – you can thank God in prayer and I do, but fate holds the key to the whys and the wherefores in life and no one will change my mind on that.

A stone monument for the Royal Ulster Rifles.

The monument was moved to Ballymena in Northern Ireland.

THE EPILOGUE

National Service

When World War II began, on 3rd September 1939, the Military training Act was replaced by National Services (Armed Forces) Act. This meant that all men aged18 to 41 years old were conscripted into the armed forces.

After the war, conscription was transformed by the National Services Act 1948. From 1st January 1949, males aged 17 to 21 years old were to serve in the armed forces for 18 months, and remain on the reserve list for 4 years.

In October 1950, due to the British involvement in the Korean War, the National Service period was extended to 2 years and the reserve period was reduced by six months.

The lead up to the war in Korea

In 1905 the Japanese ruled over Korea and the Japanese culture was forced onto the Korean population. When Japan entered World War II, the Korean people were forced to help the Japanese war effort.

When the war was over an international meeting took place called the Potsdam Conference. At this meeting it was decided that Korea should be split in two at the 38th parallel and North Korea became a communist country.

In 1950 due to a financial crisis the US decided to axe its Korean Aid Bill and cut off all aid to South Korea.

North Korea was run by Kim il-Sung who wished to unite the two Korean nations. Kim il-Sung received support from Russia.

With Russian tanks and ammunition the North Korea's People's Army (NKPA) crossed the 38th parallel in a full scale attack. Without an effective army South Korea was quickly overwhelmed and before the western allies could respond the South Korean capital Seoul was taken. The NKPA quickly moved south until only the land around the southern town of Pusan (Now Busan) remained in the capitalist hands.

Thank you for reading this far and I do hope you enjoyed it.

Finally, if you have enjoyed this book, please consider leaving a two sentence review on Amazon.

Many thanks.

Printed in Poland
by Amazon Fulfillment
Poland Sp. z o.o., Wrocław